Save Your Energy

Home Energy-Saving Solutions

Second Edition

James Symanski, Jr., P.E., MBA

Andréa M. Meyer-Symanski, MA

Morning Tea Press, LLC

Publisher's Note

This publication is designed to provide accurate and authoritative information in regard to the subject matter covered. It is sold with the understanding that the publisher is not engaged in rendering engineering, architectural, financial, or other professional services. If expert assistance is needed, the services of a competent professional should be sought.

For Elizabeth.

Table of Contents

Preface

If you're like many Americans, you pay nearly $2,200[i] in energy bills every year and you're at a loss as to how you can reduce that amount.

Let's take a look at how an "average" American family uses energy. Meet Joe and Sue.

Joe and Sue wake up around 5:30AM to get ready for work. The entire house is warm because the heater has been working hard all night to keep it that way. They start turning on lights in every room that they enter, leaving them on out of habit.

Joe goes into the bathroom and turns the shower on so it will be running hot when he's ready. He brushes his teeth and shaves, leaving the faucet running the whole time.

Sue turns up the heat because she likes it nice and toasty during her shower. It doesn't help that Joe always opens a window after his shower to help get rid of the fog on the mirror in the bathroom.

While they are getting ready, coffee is brewing in the kitchen and the coffee maker's pot warmer will keep the coffee nice and hot all day long.

Sue wakes the baby in order to get her ready for daycare. The room is quite warm because they have a space heater running all the time. She leaves the baby monitor turned on even though they don't need it during the day.

Running late getting out the door, they leave several lights and the heat on in the house. They also turn the porch light on so they can see where they walk.

When Joe comes home from work, he opens the door into their warm and toasty house. He turns on the TV and leaves it on for the rest of the evening.

As they make dinner, they discuss their day and it doesn't cross their minds to put lids on their pots to help the food cook faster.

Sue spilled something on her shirt at work, so she throws it into the clothes washer with the baby's dirty outfit from that day and uses the hot water setting to help remove the stain. When she puts it into the dryer, she is thinking about tomorrow's meeting and she forgets to clean the lint filter.

Joe opens the family's energy bill and wonders why it is over $200 for that month.

Introduction

"Waste is worse than loss. The time is coming when every person who lays claim to ability will keep the question of waste before him constantly. The scope of thrift is limitless."

- Thomas A. Edison[ii]

With global energy demand growing at an alarming rate, many areas of the world are already facing energy crises. As a homeowner, you can protect yourself and enjoy several benefits by reducing energy usage.

Less Cost. Let's face it, no one enjoys paying their energy bill. It's money that could easily be used elsewhere. By reducing your energy demand, you'll be keeping money in your pocket. More importantly, since a large percentage of energy comes from imported oil, reducing energy demand helps keep money in the United States.

Less Risk. Homeowners tied to public utility services are at the mercy of the prices set by their energy provider(s). As demand increases, it is likely that providers will continue to increase customer utility rates. Reducing demand reduces the risk of significantly higher energy bills in the long run.

Improve National Security. According to the Energy Information Agency (EIA), "In 2009, net imported energy accounted for 24 percent of all energy consumed."[iii] 44%[iv] of that energy comes from OPEC countries[v], several of which are classified by the State Department as dangerous or unstable.[vi] Because of this, the U.S. places itself at the mercy of those nations for not only its energy, but its livelihood. If we reduce our energy needs at the individual level, national demand will decrease and so will the amount of energy imports, reducing the possibility of market manipulation by potentially unfriendly foreign governments.

Protect the Environment. Our use of natural resources, like coal and oil, is causing everlasting effects to the environment. From local land destruction to oil spills and climate change, we are learning that the more energy we use the more it negatively impacts our planet.

Chapter 1

Year-Round Energy Saving Ideas

While seasonal temperature changes can have a major effect on energy usage, there are some essential steps a homeowner can take to save energy year-round.

From increasing insulation to turning off electronics when not in use, every small step can add up to big, year-round savings.

Average Home Energy Usage

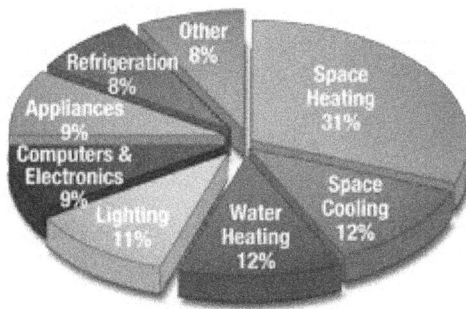

(Photo courtesy of energysavers.gov)[vii]

Energy Saving Idea #1

Eliminate Vampire Devices

Don't let electronics suck money from your budget. Many electronic devices use energy even when they are turned off, earning them the nickname of "vampire" devices for their ability to suck energy around the clock.

Common vampire devices include televisions, network routers, DVD players, home audio systems, and cell phone chargers. According to the EPA, the average home wastes nearly $100 a year needlessly powering devices that are turned off or in standby mode. The only way to know for sure that a device is not using energy when turned off is to unplug it.

An easier option is to plug all electronics into surge protectors and turn the surge protectors off when not needed, especially at night before bedtime. Using a surge protector has the added benefit of protecting electronics from power surges.

Taking the fangs out of vampire devices can save you big bucks on your energy bills.

Energy Saving Exercise

Walk around your home and identify ten potential vampire devices.

List your ten vampire devices below.

1. _____

2. _____

3. _____

4. _____

5. _____

6. _____

7. _____

8. _____

9. _____

10. _____

Hint: *When devices are turned off, look for lights, listen for sounds, and feel for heat coming from the power adapter. These are all signs that a device is using energy.*

Energy Saving Idea #2

Set Water Heater to 120° F

Tired of seeing your money drip down the drain? A no-cost fix that will save hundreds of dollars in the long run is to reduce your water heater's temperature to 120° Fahrenheit.

Many water heaters are set well above where they need to be, sometimes as much as fifty degrees too high. This not only wastes energy but also poses a safety hazard.

If your water heater has a digital thermostat, adjusting will be easy. If not, try using a thermometer to measure the temperature of the hot water coming out of a faucet. If it's hotter than 120° F, manually adjust the water heater and check the temperature again in a few hours. This may take a few attempts, but the effort will be worth it when you see next month's energy bill.

Depending on your water heater's age and usage, this adjustment can save up $100 a year.

Did you know?

According to the Center for Disease Control, boiling water is the most readily available way for homeowners to kill germs and bacteria.[viii] However, it is not possible to wash your hands under such hot water (212° F). Instead, use warm water and soap to clean hands and dishes. When washing hands, your goal should be to wash soil and germs off of the skin, not to kill the germs and bacteria.

Did you know?

According to USA Today, there are approximately 112,000 emergency room visits each year as a result of hot water scalding.[ix]

Energy Saving Idea #3

Replace Incandescent with CFL Bulbs

If you do not want to sit in the dark but want the energy bills of someone who does, try switching to compact fluorescent light bulbs. Compact fluorescent bulbs, also known as CFLs, use fluorescent technology to provide the same amount of light as incandescent bulbs but use up to 80% less energy and last up to three times longer.

CFLs are different than the dreary fluorescent light tubes of the past. Today's CFL bulbs provide the familiar cozy glow you would expect from an incandescent bulb, so you do not have to compromise light quality for efficiency. Switching from a 100-Watt incandescent to a 23-Watt CFL can save up to $77 over the life of the bulb.

Many states offer rebates for the purchase of CFLs, available as a reduction in the purchase price of the bulbs. When it comes time to dispose of your CFL bulbs, contact your local recycling center for options.

Light Bulb Comparison Guide[x]

Compare bulbs of similar output.

Incandescent	CFL	LED
40W	8W	6.7W
60W	12W	10W
100W	20W	16.7W

(Note: Chart based on average bulb output. Bulb output will vary depending on manufacturer and materials used.)

Many factors should go into light bulb selection. Below are some terms that will help you choose the best bulb for your needs.

Lumens – Light energy (brightness) emitted from a light source.

Color Rendering Index (CRI) – The numerical description of a bulb's ability to help the user differentiate colors using that light source.

Color Temperature (CT) – Description of a bulb's color output, ranging from "cool" white or blue to "warm," which appears as orange or red.

Energy Saving Idea #4

Wash Laundry in Cold Water

Though doing laundry may be a necessary evil, wasting energy doesn't need to be. An often overlooked area for energy savings is the water used in washing machines. According to the Department of Energy, 90% of energy used by washing machines goes into heating the water needed for each wash. You can save energy by using cold water instead.

Cold water detergents cost about the same as regular laundry detergents and studies show that they perform just as well as warm and hot water detergents. All the steps to using cold water detergents are the same, except turning the washer's dial to a cold water setting.

Considering the hundreds of laundry loads a typical household does every year, the savings can really add up. Get an extra bang for your buck by using an Energy Star-rated high efficiency (HE) washer, which not only saves energy but also water and detergent.

Did you know?

Based on data from a time-use survey by the Bureau of Labor Statistics, American households spend over 8.3 hours doing laundry every week.[xi]

Front-load washing machines help save energy and water.
(Photo courtesy of EnergyStar.gov)

Did you know?

Front load washing machines use, on average, 50% less water and 37% less energy than top-loading machines.[xii]

Energy Saving Idea #5

Use Energy Star Appliances

Your appliances could be devouring your energy budget. Appliances tend to be the most expensive purchases we make for our homes, but we often forget how much it costs to run them. That's where Energy Star comes in. Buying Energy Star-rated appliances saves money in the long run.

The federal government created the Energy Star program to help consumers identify the most energy efficient products available. The program sets product specifications that ensure appliances meet strict standards for energy savings, performance, and price. Any products that meet those standards earn the Energy Star.

An added bonus to purchasing Energy Star products is that many states offer rebates and tax incentives for Energy Star purchases, further reducing the overall cost. The Energy Star program covers 41 categories, so whether you're in need of a refrigerator, washing machine, or clothes dryer, you're sure to have some efficient models to choose from.

Energy-Saving Exercise

Call your local utility companies and ask them if they offer rebates for Energy Star appliances.

Record your results below.

Energy Provider(s)

Rebates offered:

_____

_____

_____

Water Provider

Rebates offered:

_____

_____

_____

Note: Energy Provider may be more than one company.

Energy Saving Idea #6

Turn Lights Off When Not Needed

It's time to shed some light on energy waste. On average, over a quarter of a home's energy is used on lighting alone. Unfortunately, a large part of that is wasted energy. To save big on your energy bills, always turn off lights when not needed.

Lighting technology has come a long way, making light bulbs and fixtures more efficient than ever. Regardless, if a light is on when it's not needed, that is wasted energy.

To make energy-saving effortless when it comes to turning off lights, consider installing daylight sensors, motion sensors, or timers to make the savings automatic. These devices identify the need for lighting without much, if any, human interaction. A simple daylight sensor can save over $35 per year, depending on the lamp's wattage and usage.

This is one of the oldest energy saving tricks in the book, but also one of the most effective.

Forming a New Habit

There is a lot of disagreement as to how long, exactly, it takes to form a new habit. Experience shows that forming a new habit often takes as little as seven days. That means to start a new, good habit you'll have to repeat it seven times for it to stick. Try this exercise:

Energy-Saving Exercise

For the next seven nights, before going to bed, walk around your home and do the following:

- Make sure all lights are turned off.
- Set thermostat to a comfortable temperature for sleeping.
- Close all blinds and curtains to keep hot or cool air in.
- Turn off all power strips to stop vampire energy waste.

If necessary, leave a note on your nightstand to remind you to do this every night.

Energy Saving Idea #7

Install Energy Efficient Windows

Don't let the chill of winter or heat of summer ruin your day. Windows are one of the biggest contributors to energy loss in a home. To reduce window heat loss, install energy efficient windows whenever possible.

Standard, single-pane windows have only one thin piece of glass, which doesn't provide much protection or insulation between the inside of a home and the outdoors. Energy efficient windows tend to have at least two panes of glass, or similar material, and a layer of air or neutral gas to provide additional insulation. This makes it much harder for heat to flow through the window.

According to the U.S. Department of Energy, an average household can save up to $293 on annual energy bills by installing energy efficient windows. When buying new or replacement windows, look for the Energy Star label and seek the assistance of a qualified professional for proper installation advice.

Important Window Characteristics[xiii]

Things to look for when buying a window:

U-Value – The rating of how quickly a window transfers heat. A relatively lower number means the window is more efficient than other windows.

Solar Heat Gain Coefficient (SHGC) – This number represents how much solar radiation a window blocks. Climate is the most important factor in selecting SHGC. In cold climates, use a low SHGC to allow more of the sun's heating rays in. In hot climates, a high SHGC will reduce cooling needs.

Air Leakage – The rate at which air can flow through a window and its frame while it is closed. Obviously, the purpose of having a window is to stop air flow, so low air leakage should be preferred.

Visible Transmittance (VT) – This term describes how much visible light the window allows into your home. In most cases, a high VT will be preferable to allow plenty of light in. If you have problems with glare, consider a lower VT.

Energy Saving Idea #8

Use Proper Refrigerator/Freezer Temperatures

That frozen pork in your freezer just might be hogging all your energy. If your freezer or refrigerator temperatures are set too cold, they are likely wasting energy and costing you money. Save yourself some dough by setting temperatures to recommended levels.

The ideal refrigerator temperature for ensuring food safety and saving energy is anywhere between 37 and 40 degrees Fahrenheit. In the freezer, aim for a temperature between 0 and 5 degrees Fahrenheit. Anything colder will waste energy.

Not sure how cold your refrigerator or freezer is? Try placing a small thermometer in each and check it after the door has been closed for five minutes.

In addition to setting your refrigerator and freezer to the recommended temperatures, be sure to look for the Energy Star label when purchasing a new refrigerator. Compared to older models, energy star-rated refrigerators can save their owners up to $200 per year.

Energy Saving Exercise

Set your refrigerator to a recommended energy-saving temperature.

Step 1. Locate a small thermometer that can safely be used in a refrigerator and freezer.

Step 2. Place the thermometer into your refrigerator for five minutes.

Step 3. Record temperature: _____ ° F

Step 4. Refrigerator temperature should be between 37-40° F. Adjust refrigerator thermostat, if necessary.

Step 5. Wait 30 minutes, then repeat steps one through four as many times as needed.

** Repeat the above exercise for your freezer. Freezer temperature should be between 0-5° F. **

Energy Saving Idea #9

Install Faucet Aerators

Don't let money wash down the drain. Water heating accounts for up to 20% of home energy consumption. To save money on water and energy, install aerators in your sink faucets.

Faucet aerators reduce the amount of water flowing from faucets by mixing air with the water. Less water flow means less water wasted. If using hot water, the savings are in both water and energy.

Faucet aerators vary in size from 0.5 to 2.2 Gallons Per Minute (GPM). Bathroom sinks are ideal for a 0.5 GPM faucet aerator and 2.2 GPM aerators are sufficient for laundry room or mud room sinks. For the kitchen sink, a 1.5 GPM aerator works for filling pots and jugs.

The beauty of faucet aerators is that you probably won't even notice a difference in the stream of water, but the savings on energy and water bills can add up to over $60 per year.

Faucet aerators inject air bubbles into the water stream to reduce water waste. (Photo Courtesy of EPA.gov)[xiv]

Things to remember:

Faucet aerators can save you up to $60 each, per year.

"We can survive as a population only if we conserve, develop sustainably, and protect the world's resources."

- Dame Silvia Cartwright, Former Governor-General of New Zealand[xv]

Energy Saving Idea #10

Install Low-Flow Shower Heads

It's time to wash away some of the waste from your energy bills. According to the U.S. Energy Information Administration, households use up to 20% of their energy to heat water. A large portion of that hot water gets used in the shower. Install low-flow shower heads to help save both water and energy.

An inefficient shower head can use up to 5.5 gallons per minute, much of which is waste. Efficient shower heads use less than 2.5 gallons per minute and can reduce shower water usage by up to 60% without sacrificing performance. Since we use energy to heat the hot water in our homes, any reduction in the use of hot water will equate to a reduction in both water and energy bills.

There are two types of water-saving shower heads: laminar flow and aerating. Consult a home improvement specialist to see which one is right for you.

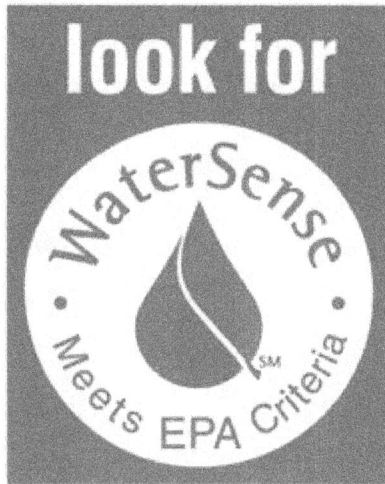

Look for the EPA's WaterSense label when purchasing showerheads.

Did you know?

"If every household in the United States installed WaterSense labeled showerheads, we could save more than $1.5 billion in water utility bills and more than 250 billion gallons of water annually, which could supply more than 2.5 million U.S. homes with their water needs for a year. In addition, we could avoid about $2.5 billion in energy costs for heating water."

– U.S. EPA[xvi]

Energy Saving Idea #11

Clean Dryer Lint Filters before Every Use

While it has yet to be proven that clothes dryers eat socks, we know for a fact that dryers have the potential to eat energy. Most of that energy is used to heat and circulate air, as well as spinning the tumbler. A dirty lint filter can reduce your dryer's efficiency by up to 30%.[xvii] To save money, be sure to clean your dryer's lint filter before every use.

Although most dryers use similar amounts of energy when used properly, a clogged lint filter reduces airflow, increasing how hard the motor must work. This results in wasted energy, extended drying times, and increased wear and tear. According to a report from the U.S. Consumer Product Safety Commission, dirty lint filters also increase the risk of fire.[xviii]

Keeping your dryer's lint filter clean is an easy way to save up to $40 per year on your energy bill while also preventing fires.[xix]

Things to remember:

Clean your dryer's lint filter
before every use.

Did you know?

Dryer lint can be composted and used with other compostable materials to fertilize your garden. Simply add it to your compost pile with other organic matter and, once composted, the lint will provide valuable nutrients to plants.

Things to remember:

Dirty lint filters can reduce
dryer efficiency by up to 30%.

Energy Saving Idea #12
Stop Drafts beneath Doors

Drafts don't just give you chills; they can also drain your wallet. If a door doesn't have adequate seals, it could be letting warm or cool air out. To save energy, block any gaps between doors and floors.

According to the U.S. Department of Energy, an average of 31% of a home's energy is used for heating, while 12% is used for cooling.[xx] With all that energy at stake, it's important to seal any gaps or leaks that may allow conditioned air to escape. While the gap under a door allows the door to swing freely, it takes a toll on your home's energy usage.

There are numerous options for blocking drafts under doors, including specialized products that can be used temporarily or installed permanently. A cost-saving option is to roll up a towel and place it at the base of the door whenever heating or cooling systems are on.

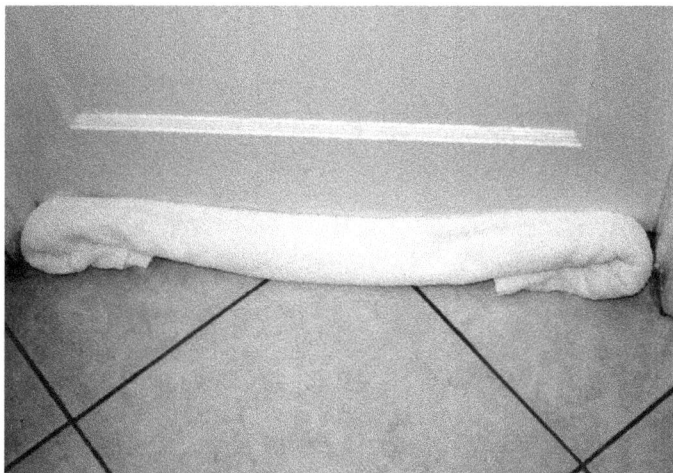

A rolled towel can help block drafts beneath doors, reducing the amount of heat lost from the room.

Things to remember:

Space heating comprises, on average, 31% of a home's energy usage.

Energy Saving Idea #13

Close Laptop Lids When Not in Use

Leaving a laptop computer open not only entices you to spend more time on your computer, but it could also be wasting energy. According to the U.S. Department of Energy, almost 10% of a home's energy budget is used on computers and electronics.[xxi] One easy way to save energy is to always close laptop computer lids when not in use.

Laptop computers, though much more efficient than desktop versions, still consume 50 watts of energy, or more, when in use.[xxii] However, when shut down or in sleep mode, the laptop computer uses 3 watts or less. That difference can add up to over $50 per year in energy costs.

To save even more energy with laptop computers, make sure your laptop is Energy Star-rated and use the power saver mode whenever possible. Also be sure to turn off peripheral devices, such as printers, speakers, and scanners, when not in use.

Average Computer Energy Usage[xxiii]

Desktop PC (CPU Only) - 120 Watts

Computer Monitor – 150 Watts

Laptop PC – 50 Watts

Netbook PC – 20 Watts [xxiv]

Ways to save energy with computers:

- Purchase an ENERGY STAR®-rated computer
- Prefer netbook and laptop PCs over desktop PCs
- Turn off network adapters when not in use
- Turn off peripheral devices when not needed
- Use "Power Saver" mode
- Dim screen when possible

Things to remember:

Laptop and Netbook PCs use up to 92% less energy than desktop PCs.

Energy Saving Idea #14

Use Microwave Oven for Heating Food

There is good reason why microwave ovens are one of the best inventions of the 20th century. Microwave ovens not only cook food faster, but also use less energy than stovetops and ovens. Next time you need to heat your dinner or steam some vegetables, consider using your microwave to save energy.

According to Flex Your Power, California's statewide energy efficiency outreach campaign, microwave ovens use 33% less energy than convection ovens and 66% less energy than conventional ovens.[xxv] This happens because the radio waves used in microwave ovens heat by exciting the atomic particles in your food. This is one of the most efficient ways to heat food.

Appliances make up 17% of the average home's energy consumption, with stovetops and ovens being two of the major contributors to that consumption.[xxvi] By using a microwave to heat food, you can take a big chunk out of your energy bills.

Did you know?

There are three forms of heat transfer: Conduction, Convection, and Radiant heating.

Conduction involves the transfer of heat from molecule to molecule in solid, or semi-solid, objects.

Convection occurs when a heated liquid or gas transfers heat to an object.

Radiant heating results when certain wavelengths of energy exist, transferring heat energy from one object to other nearby objects.

Test Your Energy Knowledge

Fill in the blanks below with 'conduction,' 'convection,' or 'radiant.'

1. A loaf of bread baking in an oven is an example of _____ heating.

2. A hand becoming cold while holding on to a metal railing is an example of _____ heating.

3. If a dark object becomes hot when in the sun, but not in the shade, this is an example of _____ heating.

Year-Round Energy Saving Ideas

Energy Saving Idea #15

Use Lids When Cooking

Put a lid on energy waste. According to the U.S. Department of Energy, the average home spends over $75 a year on energy for cooking.[xxvii] That number can easily be slashed by applying a few basic principles when cooking. One of the easiest ways to save energy in the kitchen is to always use a lid when cooking on the stovetop.

Using a lid can result in big savings. The Arizona Public Service published a report that states using a lid when cooking can increase efficiency by 8-14%.[xxviii] To maximize savings, cover and simmer foods and liquids. A simmer uses less energy than a rolling boil and cooks food just as fast.

If you're worried about the pot boiling over, purchase clear lids and keep an eye on pots while they cook. Another benefit of cooking with lids is that the lids will reduce cooking splatter and kitchen clean up time.

From the Energy Lab

In an experiment conducted by Bill Nye "The Science Guy" on his television program, he showed that when boiling water in two separate pots, a pot with its lid on will retain up to twenty degrees more heat at the boiling point than a pot without a lid. He suggests that if every household in America were to use a lid when boiling water just one time, the nation would save over $2.2M. [xxix]

Other ways to save energy when heating water...

1. Use an electric kettle.
2. Heat water in the microwave.
3. Add salt to water to lower the boiling point.

Things to remember:

Using a lid when cooking food can cut energy used by up to 14%.

Energy Saving Idea #16
Wash Only Full Laundry Loads

Laundry day may seem perpetual, but wasting energy doesn't have to be. According to the Department of Energy, the average family does more than 400 loads of laundry every year.[xxx] The annual energy cost for all those loads can add up to over $423 if done incorrectly. To save energy when doing laundry, always wash full loads.

Washers and dryers tend to use about the same amount of energy whether or not they are full. The benefit to washing full loads is that you'll have to wash fewer loads. Fewer loads equate to less work the washing machine and dryer will have to do.

Not only will full loads reduce energy usage, but you'll also save water and time. An additional way to save energy and water is to purchase a front-loading washer, which can use up to 75% less water and 85% less energy than a top-loading washer.[xxxi]

Energy Saving Exercise

Determine the recommended load size for your home's washing machine.

OPTION #1

1. If available, read your washing machine owner's manual and find the recommended load size.
2. Record your results.

_____

OPTION #2

1. If owner's manual is not available, find your washing machine brand and model.
   a. Brand: _____
   b. Model: _____
2. Call the manufacturer's customer service number and ask them the recommended load size for your model.
3. Record your results.

_____

Energy Saving Idea #17

Use Natural Lighting When Possible

The sun does more than give you a tan; it can also help reduce your energy bills. Natural light from the sun can be used to brighten and warm a space, reducing the need for additional lighting. Use natural lighting whenever possible to save energy.

The sun can provide up to 5,000 lumens per square foot, which is equivalent to about three 100-watt incandescent light bulbs[xxxii] making natural lighting a more efficient and cost effective way to light a space in the daytime.[xxxiii] Since direct sunlight can often be too bright, consider installing sheer curtains on windows to soften the light and help diffuse it throughout the room.

Maximize natural lighting by painting walls light colors and keeping window areas clear of objects that may block the incoming light. If you're planning to build or remodel a home, consider installing energy efficient skylights, dormer windows, or rooftop sunlight collectors.

Energy Saving Concept

Utilizing natural lighting while reducing window-related heat loss (and gain) can be a delicate balancing act. Homeowners should strive to install as many windows as possible so that their home will require very little electrical lighting during daylight hours, but be cautious not to install too many windows.

An excellent way to limit the effects of this tradeoff is to install thermally-insulated windows and use draperies to trap conditioned temperatures inside the home at night.

Things to remember:

The sun provides free light and heat!

Energy Saving Idea #18

Use Ceiling Fans to Circulate Air

When someone tells you ceiling fans help save energy, that's not just hot air. Central heating and cooling systems get air to a room, but they're not always good at distributing that air throughout the room. Use ceiling fans whenever possible, to help circulate conditioned air and save energy.

Ceiling fans circulate air and ensure even temperature distribution. In the summer time, set your ceiling fans to blow air down. This helps cool the skin and allows you to raise your thermostat a few degrees without impacting comfort. In the winter, reverse the fan so it blows air up, pushing accumulated hot air down from the ceiling at the edges of the room.

When selecting ceiling fans, always look for the Energy Star label. According to Home Energy Magazine Online, ceiling fans with light kits use approximately 320 kWh per year, whereas Energy Star models use only 120 kWh.[xxxiv]

Ceiling fans help circulate air, reducing the need for air conditioning. (Photo Credit: James Symanski, Jr.)[xxxv]

Did you know?

Wind chill refers to the cooling effect that occurs as air moves across a surface. The faster air moves across the skin, the faster it can remove heat from the body. In situations where air moisture levels are low, the resultant evaporation of moisture from the skin helps cool the skin even faster.

Did you know?

"If you use air conditioning, a ceiling fan will allow you to raise the thermostat setting about 4°F with no reduction in comfort" – EnergySavers.gov[xxxvi]

Energy Saving Idea #19
Properly Insulate Attics

Dark corners and spiders aren't the only scary things in your attic. Attic air leaks and inadequate insulation may be driving up your energy bills. To save energy, make sure your attic has appropriate insulation.

Attic insulation plays a vital role in protecting your home from heat loss. Its insulating properties slow the flow of heat from the conditioned living spaces below. The thickness of the insulation will determine its R-value, or ability to slow the flow of heat. Recommended R-values depend on a home's location, but generally range between R30-R60.

There are several different types of insulation, the most common of which are loose fill and fiberglass batts or blankets. Either type is fine for most attics, though loose fill insulation may require special equipment to install.

According to the U.S. Department of Energy, proper air sealing and insulation can reduce heating and cooling costs by up to 20%.[xxxvii]

Recommended Attic Insulation Levels

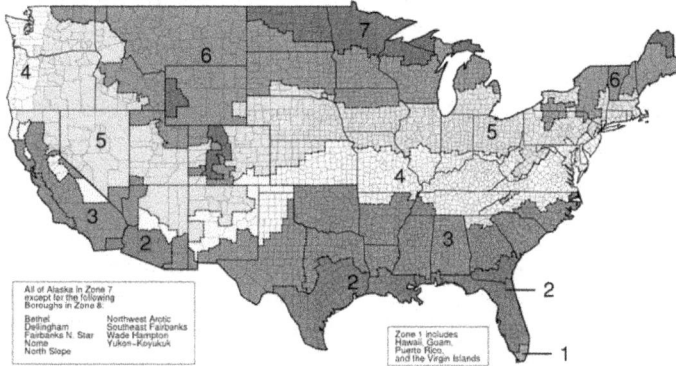

Zone	Recommended Attic Insulation
1	R30 to R49
2	R30 to R60
3	R30 to R60
4	R38 to R60
5 to 8	R49 to R60

(Courtesy: EnergyStar.gov)[xxxviii]

Energy Saving Idea #20

Use Automatic Lighting Controls

Tired of running around the house, turning lights off after your family? Automatic lighting controls take comfort and energy savings to a whole new level. Installing automatic lighting controls will save you time and energy.

There are several options for automatic lighting controls, including motion sensors, daylight sensors and timers. Each turns lights on and off based on specific conditions such as room occupancy, daylight levels, and pre-set times. Sensors also draw very little energy. A study done by Australia's Ministerial Council on Energy found that motion sensors in standby mode draw only 0.2-1.5 watts.[xxxix]

A study published by IEEE (Institute of Electrical and Electronics Engineers) showed that lighting energy costs can be reduced up to 50% by installing automatic lighting controls.[xl] Since the average household spends 11% of its energy budget on lighting, installing automatic light controls can take a chunk out of your energy bill.[xli]

Automatic Lighting Controls

Automatic lighting controls take the thought out of lighting. Make your energy savings simple with these solutions...

Use Daylight Sensors for:

- All outdoor lighting
- Lighting near windows and skylights

Use Timers for:

- Lights used with a specific schedule (i.e. living room lights, porch lights, holiday decorative lights, etc.)
- Electronic devices (wireless internet routers, cell phone chargers, etc.)

Use Motion Sensors for:

- All security-type lighting
- Porch, walkway, and driveway lighting
- Garage lighting
- Lighting in small, lightly occupied rooms (i.e. laundry rooms, closets, etc.)

Energy Saving Idea #21

Avoid Pre-Rinsing Dishes

If you're still rinsing dishes before putting them into the dishwasher, you may be wasting time and money. Contrary to the popular belief that pre-rinsing is necessary to get clean dishes, pre-rinsing is often not required.

The myth that dishes must be rinsed before being placed into the dishwasher started with the earliest version of the dishwasher, which would clog easily when food matter got caught in the drain. Since then, dishwasher manufacturers have been adding ways to avoid this problem. Most dishwashers now have built in food disposals to grind food matter and prevent it from clogging drains.

You'll still want to remove heavy soil from dishes before putting them into the dishwasher, but small food particles pose little danger. As always, you should check the manufacturer's instructions prior to using a dishwasher. If pre-rinsing is not required, you could save yourself hundreds of gallons of water every year.

Did you know?

Compared to hand washing dishes, over the course of a year an Energy Star-rated dishwasher can save you:[xlii]

- Up to $431 in energy and water.
- 230 hours of personal time.
- 5,000 gallons of water.

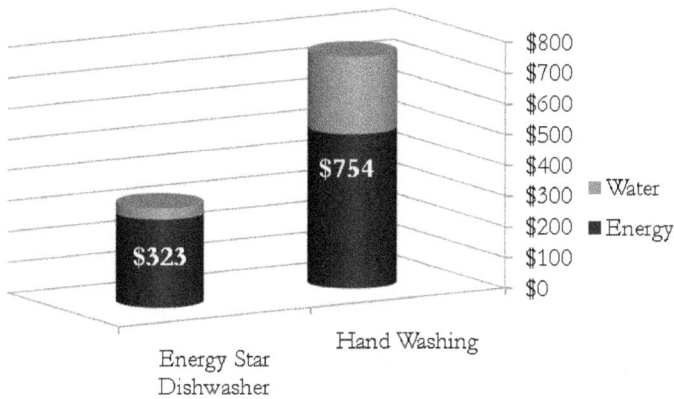

Using an Energy Star-rated dishwasher can save homeowners up to $431 a year when compared to hand washing. (Source: EnergyStar.gov) [xliii]

Energy Saving Idea #22

Insulate Heating and Cooling Ducts

If your heating and cooling bills seem to be out of control, your ducts may be to blame. Duct insulation helps keep conditioned air hot or cold while moving throughout home. To save big on your energy bills, make sure duct insulation is present and adequate.

A properly insulated duct typically has two inches or more of standard insulation protecting it from unconditioned air in attics, basements, and crawl spaces. Without that insulation, the air travelling through the ducts will quickly lose or gain heat depending on the difference between conditioned air temperatures and outside temperatures. This heat transfer makes your air handling systems work harder and wastes energy.

Most duct insulation can be purchased at home improvement stores and installed by a homeowner. Hard-to-reach or elaborate duct systems may require a professional contractor, but the insulation will likely pay for itself within a year or two.

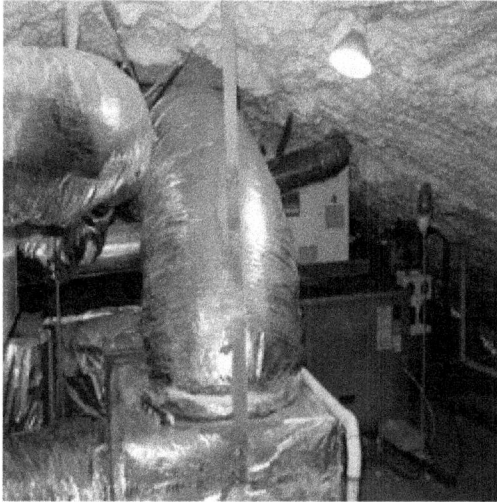

What this lacks in looks, it makes up for in warm and cool comfort! Note the insulated ducts and spray-foam insulated surfaces. (Photo courtesy of epa.gov)

Things to remember:

While most duct insulation may be installed by homeowners, insulation near high-temperature heat sources should be installed by a professional.

Energy Saving Idea #23

Keep Windows and Doors Closed

Unless you live in a barn, it's never a good idea to leave windows and doors open while heating or cooling systems are on. Your heating and cooling systems work hard to condition your home's air and make it comfortable. Don't let that hard work go to waste. Always close windows and doors to keep conditioned air inside your home.

According to the Department of Energy, the average home uses 43% of its energy for heating and cooling.[xliv] If just one window were left open, the amount of energy needed to condition the air in that space could easily quadruple. This energy loss can be attributed to air flowing directly out of the space, as well as heat transfer through the now un-insulated surface.

Get the whole family involved by having a hunt for open doors and windows. This can help save hundreds, or even thousands, of dollars each year.

Energy Saving Exercise

Next time you turn on your heating or cooling system, complete the following steps.

1. Walk around your home, looking for open windows and exterior doors.
2. Ensure vents are clear of objects that may impede airflow.
3. Close curtains and blinds to help reduce heat transfer through windows. (Except south-facing windows on cold, sunny days)
4. Close vents in, and doors to, unoccupied rooms.

Things to remember:

Open windows and doors can quadruple energy costs.

Chapter 2

Winter Energy Saving Ideas

"Now is the winter of our discontent"
– William Shakespeare

Winter is the time of year when most people feel the pain of their energy bills. Cold winter nights can strain heating systems and burn heating fuel nearly non-stop. Fewer daylight hours means more electrical lighting needs.

Most of the energy used during winter months goes to space heating. That's why it's important to focus on improving insulation and heating system efficiency before the cold of winter sets in.

In this chapter, you'll learn some tricks for doing just that, as well as a few other ways to save energy during the winter months.

Winter Temperatures

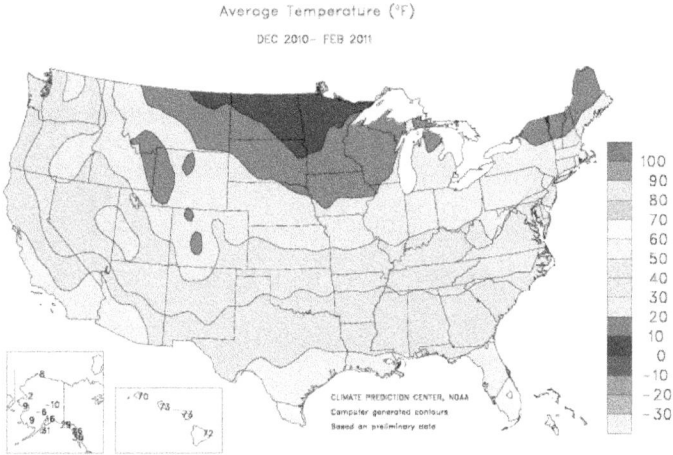

Average temperatures for Dec. 2010 – Feb. 2011. (Courtesy of the National Oceanographic and Atmospheric Administration)[xlv]

Extreme Minimum Temperature (°F)

DEC 2010- FEB 2011

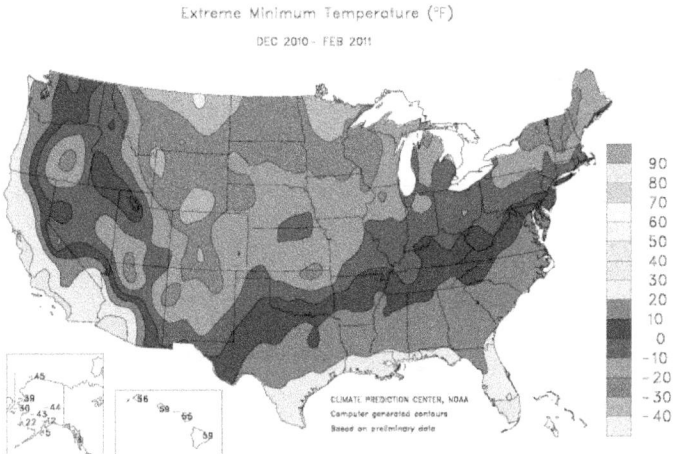

Extreme minimum temperatures for Dec. 2010 – Feb. 2011. (Courtesy of the National Oceanographic and Atmospheric Administration)[xlvi]

Winter Energy Saving Ideas   55

Energy Saving Idea #24

Use Programmable Thermostats

Maximize your heating dollars with precision this winter. According to the Department of Energy, heating makes up almost 50% of a home's winter energy bill. Programmable thermostats can help save a large portion of that energy by automatically adjusting system temperatures to correspond to a homeowner's needs.

When setting a programmable thermostat, consider reducing the temperature before bed and any time the house will be empty. There are a lot of models available, so be sure to look for the Energy Star label when shopping for a programmable thermostat. The Environmental Protection Agency awards the Energy Star label to products that are among the most efficient in their class. Some brands can be easily installed by homeowners, while others require an electrician or heating system technician.

Switching to a programmable thermostat can save homeowners up to 15% on their energy bills, which can add up to over $300 per year.

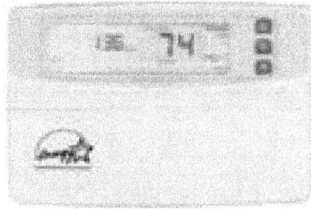

When purchasing a programmable thermostat, look for the Energy Star. (Photo courtesy of EnergyStar.gov)

Recommended Thermostat Temperatures[xlvii]

Heating Season

Occupied Rooms: 68-72°F

Unoccupied Rooms: 50-60°F

Cooling Season

Occupied Rooms: 72-76°F

Unoccupied Rooms: 80-90°F

Things to remember:

Programmable thermostats can save up to $300/year.

Energy Saving Idea #25

Use Caulk to Seal out Cold Air

Don't let money leak from your home this winter. Use caulk to seal windows, door frames, dryer vents, and any other opening that allows warm air to leak from your home. Caulk creates a solid barrier preventing air from moving through cracks and gaps in your walls.

Caulk is relatively easy to apply using a caulk gun available at hardware and home improvement stores. There are several different types of caulk available, so be sure to check that you are using the correct type for your application.

According to the EPA, caulking can help homeowners save up to 20% on annual heating bills, which is a significant return on your investment when you consider that one canister can seal two windows.

Applying caulk in your home may also make you eligible for several tax credits. For more information on tax credits and financial incentives, visit the EPA's Energy Star website.

Did you know?

Signed in January, 2007 by President George W. Bush, **Executive Order 13423** ("Strengthening Federal Environmental, Energy, and Transportation Management,") requires the federal government to reduce its energy consumption by 3% per year from 2007 to 2016.[xlviii] The purpose is to "improve energy efficiency and reduce greenhouse gas emissions."

Other parts of EO 13423 include a mandate that half of all renewable energy must come from new renewable sources, and requires fleets of vehicles to decrease their petroleum usage by 2% annually. Plug in Hybrids (PIH) must also be used where commercially available.

President Barack Obama continued the principles outlined in EO 13423 in October 2009[xlix] when he signed EO 13514, further defining the federal government's commitment to energy efficiency and conservation.

If the federal government can do all that to improve efficiency, it should be easy for homeowners to do the same with a little planning.

Energy Saving Idea #26

Close Blinds and Curtains at Night

Windows are one of the biggest culprits when it comes to heat loss in homes. According to the National Fenestration Rating Council, rooms lose up to 84% of their heat through windows. A great way to reduce this heat loss is to close blinds and curtains at night.

Closing blinds and curtains increases a window's thermal resistance factor, or R-value, by slowing airflow through gaps in window frames and also by creating an insulating layer of air between the warm room and the cold window. For maximum effectiveness, use double curtains and hang them as close to the window or wall as possible and eliminate gaps between curtain panels, the wall, and the floor.

According to the Department of Energy's Energy Efficiency and Renewable Energy Consumer Guide, closing blinds and curtains at night can reduce window heat loss by up to 25%, a potential savings of several hundred dollars per year.

For window coverings to help insulate a window, they should close completely and not have any gaps around the sides, top, or bottom of the window opening.

Things to remember:

Closing curtains and blinds can reduce window heat loss by up to 25%.

Energy Saving Idea #27

Keep Heating System Filters Clean

Pet hair, dust, and debris - your heater's air filter can be a scary sight. Keeping your air filter clean isn't just hygienic, but can also save money on energy. Clean, or replace, your heating system's air filter at least once every three months, especially during heavy use periods.

Heaters rely on air filters to clean the air flowing into the system, which not only protects the heater's mechanical components but also your health. When a filter becomes clogged, it slows air flow and can eventually lead to system failure.

Air filters are easy to clean or replace. Some models are designed to be cleaned off with a vacuum cleaner, while other filters are disposable and should be replaced by a new filter. Check your system manual for more information. Cleaning your filter every three months will keep your heating system working properly and save you a bundle of money.

Energy Saving Exercise

Locate your heating system's filter. Record the filter location, brand, and size below.

Filter location (room): _____

Filter brand: _____

Filter size: _____

Hint: *The filter is typically located near the heating system's air intake, either at the spot where air enters the intake duct or where the intake duct feeds into the heating system.*

Warning:

Do not attempt to disassemble the heating system. Filters are usually very easy for homeowners to find and replace; if you have to work to get to it, you probably weren't meant to get to it.

Energy Saving Idea #28

Use Christmas Lighting Wisely

Don't let your energy bill ruin Christmas. During the Christmas season, households can spend up to $300 more on energy than during other months. A lot of that energy goes to Christmas lights and displays. During the Christmas season, use lighting wisely to save energy.

One way to save energy with Christmas displays is by using a timer to ensure the lights only come on at sundown and turn off automatically by 9PM. Another thing to consider is using LED lights for holiday displays. LED bulbs have come a long way - they now provide a wide variety of festive colors and patterns while saving energy.

Since LED bulbs use up to 90% less energy than mini bulbs, combining the use of LED bulbs with a lighting timer can reduce Christmas lighting energy consumption by as much as 97%. The savings on your energy bill will feel like a present.

Did you know?

Since 2007, LED light bulbs have been used to decorate the National Christmas Tree at the White House.

LED light bulbs adorn the National Christmas Tree. (Photo courtesy of blogs.america.gov)[1]

Things to remember:

LED Christmas lights use up to 90% less energy than standard Christmas lights.

Energy Saving Idea #29

Use Heat Wisely

Take the chill out of cold winter weather while also saving money. According to the U.S. Department of Energy, 31% of an average home's energy is used for heating living spaces.[li] To save energy, set thermostats to recommended levels.

The recommended temperature for an occupied room or building is 68°F, health permitting. Unoccupied spaces should be no more than 55°F.[lii] An additional measure for saving energy may be to dress warmly and lower thermostats a few degrees.

For every five degree increase in thermostat temperature, a homeowner will have to pay up to 20% more in heating costs. Conversely, every five degree decrease in thermostat temperature can equate to a savings of 20%.[liii]

An easy way to save and not have to think about constantly changing the thermostat is to install a programmable thermostat. Programmable thermostats allow homeowners to adjust temperatures automatically at specified times.

Energy Saving Exercise

Take a minute to think through your home's day. Record any 'unoccupied' time periods below:

Time Period #1: _____

Time Period #2: _____

Time Period #3: _____

Time Period #4: _____

Time Period #5: _____

Next, set your thermostat to its 'unoccupied' setting during the above time periods.

Things to remember:

Heating should be set no warmer than 68°F for an occupied room and 55°F for an unoccupied room.

Energy Saving Idea #30

Install Storm Windows in Winter

If the thought of winter gives you chills, your home may be losing heat through its windows. According to the California Energy Commission, heating costs in winter can be up to 30% higher due to heat loss through windows.[liv] To reduce window heat loss, install storm windows in winter.

Storm windows not only add an additional layer of glass to slow heat loss, but they also create an air-filled gap between window surfaces. Air is one of the best insulators for protecting your home from cold outdoor temperatures. The state of California's energy efficiency campaign, Flex Your Power, estimates that storm windows can reduce window heat loss by 25-50%.[lv]

Storm windows can be purchased at most home improvement stores and easily installed by residents without needing specialized help. Considering that heating accounts for 31% of your home's annual energy usage, storm windows will quickly pay for themselves.[lvi]

Did you know?

Single-pane windows are found in many older homes, but the technology pre-dates most American homes by nearly 2000 years. Romans started using panes of glass in their windows by the first century. The Roman, single-pane windows were half an inch thick and could be opened and closed to allow air flow.

Dual-pane windows were invented in Scotland in the 1930s as a thrifty way to heat large Victorian homes and castles, which had multiple levels and one primary source of heat – a fireplace. Dual-pane, or double-glazed, windows made their way into the construction of American homes in the 1950s and have been hugely popular ever since.[lvii] They decrease thermal transfer and save energy.

Recently, there have even been triple-pane windows manufactured and sold in the U.S. Triple-pane windows provide as much insulation as one and a half inches of wall insulation.

Energy Saving Idea #31

Heat Occupied Rooms Only

If you're tired of high heating bills, it's time to take a look at where your heat is being used. Most of us only use a few rooms regularly, so why heat empty rooms? This especially applies to basements, guest bedrooms, and seldom-used bathrooms. If there is an area in your home not regularly used, consider turning off the heat or lowering the thermostat in that area to save on heating bills.

To reduce heat waste in unoccupied spaces, close heating vents and doors in those rooms. To maximize energy savings, place a rolled towel on the floor in front of the door to stop airflow. If a room has its own thermostat, turn the thermostat down to 55°F when no one is in the room.

With space heating being one of the largest contributors to the average home's energy bill, taking these small steps can significantly reduce heating bills.

Energy Saving Exercise

Determine which rooms in your home do not need to be heated. Record your results below.

Room name: _____

Room name: _____

Room name: _____

Room name: _____

Room name: _____

Room name: _____

Hint: Rooms do not need to be heated, or can be minimally heated, if they are not regularly occupied. Some common examples are unfinished basements, vacant bedrooms, and closets.

BONUS: In the rooms listed above, complete the following actions:

- Turn off heat to that room.
- Close heating vents.
- Block airflow beneath doors.

Energy Saving Idea #32

Avoid Using Space Heaters

When the cold winter chill starts setting in, you may be tempted to use a space heater. Deceptively small in size, space heaters require a lot of energy to operate. To save big on your heating bills, keep space heaters out of your home.

In most cases, using a whole-house heater is more cost effective than using space heaters. This is especially true if your home's main heating system uses natural gas, since the same amount of heat energy from natural gas is typically less expensive than heat produced from electricity.

If you must use a space heater in your home, only use one that turns on and off based on the room's temperature. In addition, close all windows and doors to the room you are heating. Since drafts will only make the space heater work harder and drive your energy bill higher, seal gaps around all windows and doors.

Energy Saving Exercise

Nighttime Energy Saving Walk-around

Walk around the outside of your home at night, looking for potential savings:

- Look for any lights left on when not needed, including interior lights.
- Look for open windows, blinds, and curtains. (Only if heater or air conditioner are on)
- Look for light shining through structural components, indicating a need for sealing.

Once you've finished your walk-around, consider the following energy saving ideas:

- Close open windows, curtains, and blinds.
- Consider using motion sensors, daylight sensors, and timers for exterior lighting needs.
- Caulk around windows, doors, or any other area with a visible gap.

Chapter 3

Summer Energy Saving Ideas

Summer is a great time for travel, picnics, and swimming. The warm air and longer days let us enjoy more time outdoors.

For all its benefits, summer provides unique challenges when it comes to saving energy. Longer days mean fewer lighting needs, but hotter temperatures require more cooling.

The majority of energy usage in homes during summer months goes to cooling living spaces. Those cooling costs don't need to bust your budget, however.

The following pages provide great ways to trim your summer energy bill and optimize the benefits of summer without sacrificing comfort or convenience.

Did you know?

High summer temperatures cost homeowners billions in cooling costs. Check out these average, summer high temperatures to see what your region can expect for high temperatures.

City	Ave. High
Atlanta, GA	89°F
Anchorage, AK	65°F
Boston, MA	82°F
Dallas, TX	96°F
Denver, CO	88°F
Detroit, MI	85°F
Honolulu, HI	89°F
Los Angeles, CA	85°F
Miami, FL	91°F
Minneapolis, MN	83°F
New York, NY	83°F
Phoenix, AZ	107°F
Sacramento, CA	94°F
St. Louis, MO	91°F
Washington, D.C.	88°F

(Source: Weather.com)

Energy Saving Idea #33

Cool Your Home Wisely

Staying cool in summer isn't always easy, but sweating over your energy bill can make summer unbearable. According to the U.S. Department of Energy, 12% of a home's annual energy needs go to keeping the home cool. You can save energy and money by using your cooling system wisely.

The recommended temperature for an occupied home in summertime is 78°F. When the home is unoccupied, raise the temperature to 85°F. According to Flex Your Power, the California statewide energy efficiency campaign, raising your thermostat just five degrees will result in a savings of up to 20% on cooling costs.

Use a programmable thermostat to automatically adjust temperatures at pre-set times. Another way to save is to raise the thermostat a few degrees and use ceiling fans to circulate the cool air. Even when the air is a bit warmer, the breeze created by a fan helps cool your skin.

In summertime, set cooling thermostats to 78°F when occupied and 85°F when unoccupied. (Photo courtesy of Nebraska State Energy Office)[lviii]

Things to remember:

Raising air conditioning thermostats to 85°F during unoccupied times can cut cooling costs by up to 20%.

Energy Saving Idea #34

Save Heat-Producing Activities for Cool Hours

When it's hot outside, your air conditioner has to work harder to cool interior spaces. Give it a hand by performing heat-producing activities during evening or morning hours.

An air conditioner's ability to transfer heat to the outdoor environment is significantly reduced during hot weather. Activities such as cooking, laundry, and even physical activity, create heat which then must be removed from the conditioned space. That removal takes more time and uses more energy when it is hot outside.

The same principle applies during the winter. Heat pumps and heaters have to work harder at night, so performing heat-producing activities during that time will help reduce the amount of work they must do. Try to cook dinner later and set clothes dryers to start after five o'clock. Later is better.

This principle is known as 'temperature differential' and applying it in daily life will help you save energy and money.

List of Heat-Producing Activities

- Baking in the oven
- Cooking on the stove
- Drying clothes
- Exercise
- Hair drying
- Ironing clothes
- Showers
- Washing clothes in hot water

Energy Saving History Lesson

During colonial times, many American households, particularly in the warmer regions, had winter kitchens and summer kitchens. The summer kitchens were separate from the main house, to keep the heat-producing activities away from the living space. Winter kitchens were located in basements, to help heat the house.[lix]

Energy Saving Idea #35

Use Blinds to Block out Summer Heat

Don't let the summer sun burn you on your energy bill. While the sun's rays can help brighten indoor spaces, direct sunlight may be causing unnecessary heat gain in your home. To reduce summer cooling costs, use blinds and curtains to block out direct sunlight.

The sun's heating rays, including infrared, ultraviolet, and visible light rays, are responsible for the heat we feel when the sun shines on our skin. Using blinds and curtains to block and diffuse sunlight will allow occupants to enjoy the benefit of natural lighting without the added heat.

An additional benefit of blocking the sun's heating rays is that it will protect furnishings and household items from fading and other damage associated with ultraviolet radiation. Another option to consider is installing special window films that block particular wavelengths of light, such as ultraviolet and infrared, from entering your home while allowing most visible light in.

Energy Saving Exercise

Around midday on a sunny day, identify windows that allow direct sunlight into your home.

Record your results below:

Location: _____

Location: _____

Location: _____

Location: _____

Location: _____

Location: _____

Once identified, close blinds to reduce the amount of direct sunlight entering the home.

Things to remember:

Install light-colored blinds to reflect both light and heat.

Epilogue

Now that Joe and Sue have read **Save Your Energy: Home Energy Saving Solutions**, they have taken a close look around their home and re-analyzed their daily routine. They've realized there is a lot they can do to save on their energy bills.

Now, when Joe and Sue wake up in the morning, they only turn on lights that need to be on. The house is warm when they get out of bed, but only because their new programmable thermostat turns the heat on fifteen minutes before their alarm sounds.

Joe no longer runs the water while he is in the bathroom. The aerating faucets and efficient shower head also help to save water and energy when the water is on.

Sue knows that the baby's room doesn't need to be heated as much as it was. They have purchased a space heater with a thermostat that they set to 70 degrees, which is only needed to supplement the house heater and ensure the baby is warm. They've also put the baby's room monitor on a timer so that it is turned off during the day.

Before Joe and Sue leave the house, they take a quick look around to make sure everything is turned off. They need not worry about turning off the heating system because the programmable thermostat will take care of that.

They also no longer have to turn on the porch light to see – their new lamp has a motion sensing option that comes on when they walk out, then turns off after they have left.

When Joe comes home from work, he only turns the television on if there is a program he would like to watch. And Sue no longer washes clothes in hot water – she purchased cold water detergent and is pleased to see it works just as well as her old detergent. She always checks the lint filter before drying clothes, and she only washes full loads.

Now that Joe and Sue have changed their habits and invested a little bit into their home's energy efficiency, they have slashed their energy bills by more than half. They are putting the extra money into a savings account to use on a vacation.

Action List

Below is a list of all the energy-saving ideas contained within this book. Place a check in the block after you've completed each energy-saving step.

☐ Turn Off Vampire Devices (Pg. 15)

☐ Set Water Heater to 120° F (Pg. 17)

☐ Replace Incandescent with CFL Bulbs (Pg. 19)

☐ Wash Laundry in Cold Water (Pg. 21)

☐ Use Energy Star Appliances (Pg. 23)

☐ Turn Lights Off When Not Needed (Pg. 25)

☐ Install Energy Efficient Windows (Pg. 27)

☐ Use Proper Refrigerator/Freezer Temperatures (Pg. 29)

☐ Install Faucet Aerators (Pg. 31)

☐ Install Low-Flow Shower Heads (Pg. 33)

☐ Clean Dryer Lint Filter before Every Use (Pg. 35)

☐ Stop Drafts beneath Doors (Pg. 37)

☐ Close Laptop Lids when not in Use (Pg. 39)

☐ Use Microwave Oven for Heating Food (Pg. 41)

☐ Use Lids When Cooking (Pg. 43)

☐ Wash Only Full Laundry Loads (Pg. 45)

☐ Use Natural Lighting When Possible (Pg. 47)

☐ Use Ceiling Fans to Circulate Air (Pg. 49)

☐ Properly Insulate Attics (Pg. 51)

☐ Use Automatic Lighting Controls (Pg. 53)

☐ Avoid Pre-Rinsing Dishes (Pg. 55)

☐ Insulate Heating and Cooling Ducts (Pg. 57)

☐ Keep Windows and Doors Closed (Pg. 59)

☐ Use Programmable Thermostats (Pg. 63)

☐ Use Caulk to Seal out Cold Air (Pg. 65)

☐ Close Blinds and Curtains at Night (Pg. 67)

☐ Keep Heating System Filters Clean (Pg. 69)

☐ Use Christmas Lighting Wisely (Pg. 71)

☐ Use Heat Wisely (Pg. 73)

☐ Install Storm Windows in Winter (Pg. 75)

☐ Heat Occupied Rooms Only (Pg. 77)

☐ Avoid Using Space Heaters (Pg. 79)

☐ Cool Your Home Wisely (Pg. 83)

☐ Save Heat-Producing Activities for Cool Hours (Pg. 85)

☐ Use Blinds to Block out Summer Heat (Pg. 87)

About the Authors

James Symanski is a registered Professional Engineer (P.E.) and Certified Energy Manager (CEM®). He is a West Point graduate and holds masters degrees in both engineering and business. A disabled combat veteran, he has been helping the federal government reduce its energy usage since leaving the military in 2009. He currently serves on the White House's Infrastructure Resilience Working Group and various other boards and committees focused on energy efficiency and sustainability.

Andréa Meyer-Symanski is an educator devoted to intelligent conservation of the nation's resources. She holds a masters degree from California State University-Fresno and has served as a professional editor, teacher, and speaker in the U.S. and abroad.

James and Andréa live with their two daughters in the Washington, D.C. metropolitan area.

Ordering Instructions

To order additional copies of this book, including bulk orders, please write to customer_support@morningteapress.com for more information.

References

ⁱhttp://www.energystar.gov/index.cfm?c=products.pr_pie

ⁱⁱhttp://www.brainyquote.com/quotes/quotes/t/thomasaed149 058.html

ⁱⁱⁱhttp://www.eia.doe.gov/aer/pdf/aer.pdf

^{iv}http://www.eia.doe.gov/aer/pdf/aer.pdf

^vhttp://www.opec.org/opec_web/en/about_us/25.htm

^{vi}http://travel.state.gov/travel/cis_pa_tw/tw/tw_1764.html

^{vii}http://www.energysavers.gov/tips/home_energy.cfm

^{viii}http://www.cdc.gov/healthywater/drinking/travel/backcount ry_water_treatment.html

^{ix}http://www.healthscout.com/ency/68/606/main.html

^xhttp://www.energysavers.gov/your_home/lighting_daylighting /index.cfm/mytopic=12030

^{xi}http://www.bls.gov/opub/mlr/2009/07/art3full.pdf

^{xii}http://www.energystar.gov/index.cfm?fuseaction=find_a_pro duct.showProductGroup&pgw_code=CW

^{xiii}http://www.energysavers.gov/your_home/windows_doors_s kylights/index.cfm/mytopic=13320

^{xiv} http://www.epa.gov/oaintrnt/images/denver_faucet.jpg

xvhttp://www.brainyquote.com/quotes/keywords/conserve.html#ixzz1HX0zXhri

xvihttp://www.epa.gov/watersense/products/showerheads.html

xviihttp://www.state.nj.us/bpu/residential/tips/

xviiihttp://www.cpsc.gov/library/foia/foia03/os/dryer.pdf

xixhttp://www.state.nj.us/bpu/residential/tips/

xxhttp://www.energysavers.gov/tips/home_energy.cfm

xxihttp://www.energysavers.gov/tips/home_energy.cfm

xxiihttp://www.energysavers.gov/your_home/appliances/index.cfm/mytopic=10040

xxiiihttp://www.energysavers.gov/your_home/appliances/index.cfm/mytopic=10040

xxivhttp://www.upenn.edu/computing/provider/docs/hardware/powerusage.html

xxvhttp://www.fypower.org/res/tools/energy_tips_results.html?tips=cooking

xxvihttp://www.energysavers.gov/tips/home_energy.cfm

xxviihttp://www.energysavers.gov/tips/appliances.cfm

xxviiihttp://www.aps-solutionsforbusiness.com/ProjectCenter/Portals/54/Cooking.pdf

xxixhttp://www.pbs.org/wgbh/nova/physics/bill-nye-cooks.html

xxxhttp://www.energystar.gov/index.cfm?fuseaction=find_a_pro

duct.showProductGroup&pgw_code=CW

xxxihttp://www.energystar.gov/index.cfm?fuseaction=clotheswas
h.display_products_html

xxxiihttp://www.efi.org/factoids/lumens.html

xxxiiihttp://www.hydroempire.com/store/hydroponic-light-
photosynthesis.php

xxxivhttp://www.homeenergy.org/consumerinfo/fans/index.php

xxxvhttp://www.energysavers.gov/seasonal/tips_summer.html

xxxvihttp://www.energysavers.gov/seasonal/tips_summer.html

xxxviihttp://www.energystar.gov/index.cfm?c=home_sealing.hm
_improvement_sealing

xxxviiihttp://www.energystar.gov/index.cfm?c=home_sealing.hm
_improvement_insulation_table

xxxixhttp://www.energyrating.gov.au/library/pubs/sb200411-
sensors.pdf

xlhttp://ieeexplore.ieee.org/Xplore/login.jsp?url=http%3A%2F
%2Fieeexplore.ieee.org%2Fiel1%2F28%2F5996%2F00231992.p
df%3Farnumber%3D231992&authDecision=-203

xlihttp://www.energysavers.gov/tips/home_energy.cfm

xliihttp://www.energystar.gov/index.cfm?c=dishwash.pr_handw
ash_dishwash

xliiihttp://www.energystar.gov/index.cfm?c=dishwash.pr_handw
ash_dishwash

xlivhttp://www.energysavers.gov/tips/home_energy.cfm

xlvhttp://www.cpc.ncep.noaa.gov/products/analysis_monitoring

/regional_monitoring/3monthusavgt.gif

[xlvi]http://www.cpc.ncep.noaa.gov/products/analysis_monitorin
g/regional_monitoring/3monthusmint.gif

[xlvii]http://www.apd.army.mil/pdffiles/r420_1.pdf

[xlviii]http://edocket.access.gpo.gov/2007/pdf/07-374.pdf

[xlix]http://www.fedcenter.gov/programs/eo13514/

[l]http://blogs.america.gov/obama/2009/12/04/christmas-at-
the-white-house/

[li]http://www.energysavers.gov/tips/home_energy.cfm

[lii]http://www.fypower.org/res/changing-habits.html

[liii]http://www.fypower.org/res/changing-habits.html

[liv]http://www.consumerenergycenter.org/home/windows/today
s_windows.html

[lv]http://www.fypower.org/res/tools/energy_tips_results.html?ti
ps=heating

[lvi]http://www.energysavers.gov/tips/home_energy.cfm

[lvii]http://www.double-glazing-
windows.com/doubleglazingwindowbenefits.php

[lviii]http://www.neo.ne.gov/neq_online/march2005/march2005.
web.htm

[lix]http://www.history.org/foundation/journal/summer07/kitch
ens.cfm

References   91

www.ingramcontent.com/pod-product-compliance
Lightning Source LLC
Chambersburg PA
CBHW070538030426
42337CB00016B/2251